Pumpkin Carving

Pumpkin Carving

Ed Palmer

Sterling Publishing Co., Inc. New York

A Sterling/Chapelle Book

For information on where to purchase specialty items in
this book please write to: Customer Service Department., 204
25th Street, Ogden, Utah 84401

A Sterling/Chapelle Book

10 9 8 7 6 5 4 3 2

Published in paperback 2001 by
Sterling Publishing Company, Inc.
387 Park Avenue South, New York, N.Y. 10016
© 1995 by Chapelle Ltd.
Distributed in Canada by Sterling Publishing
C/o Canadian Manda Group, One Atlantic Avenue, Suite 105
Toronto, Ontario, Canada M6K 3E7
Distributed in Great Britain and Europe by Chris Lloyd at Orca Book
Services, Stanley House, Fleets Lane, Poole BH15 3AJ, England.
Distributed in Australia by Capricorn Link (Australia) Pty. Ltd.
P.O. Box 704, Windsor, NSW 2756 Australia
Printed in Hong Kong
All rights reserved

Sterling ISBN 0-8069-6419-7

For Chapelle Ltd.

Owner
Jo Packham

Editor
Cherie Hanson

Staff
Malissa Boatwright
Trice Boerens
Rebecca Christensen
Holly Fuller
Holly Hollingsworth
Susan Jorgensen
Susan Laws
Amanda McPeck
Barbara Milburn
Jamie C. Pierce
Leslie Ridenour
Cindy Rooks
Cindy Stoekle
Ryanne Webster
Nancy Whitley

Photographer
Kevin Dilly
For Hazen Photography

About the Authors

Ed Palmer

I come from a family of craftspeople and thinkers, alternating by generations. Grandpa was a great cabinetmaker who spent evenings in front of the fireplace carving beautiful animals with his pocket-knife. Dad is a physicist. Grandma was a beautician and wonderful seamstress. Mom does quilts and crochets. I am somewhere in between, with an art degree and an MS in Industrial Education.

Currently I teach high school art, which is truly enjoyable because I have the opportunity to help teenagers discover, develop, and work with their creativity; they likewise influence, challenge, and enhance my creativity. As a teacher, there is the daily opportunity both to make things and to work with people.

Most of the time I consider myself to be a potter, and I do spend a considerable amount of my time making things out of clay. I have always wanted to make great and different Halloween pumpkins, and have tried out all kinds of different tools for carving them. I could never do any that I really liked until I discovered the little saw tools and learned to draw the design first, then transfer it to the pumpkin with the poking tool.

The time spent designing the patterns for this book was really fun, as was working with Evelyn and the people at Chapelle. I hope you enjoy using our patterns or adapting them to suit your own needs. I believe the role of art in life is to serve our personal expressive needs, including to amuse, entertain, challenge, educate, confront, or stimulate, both as creator and viewer. I hope this book will stimulate your creativity and help serve your expressive needs.

Happy carving!

Evelyn Kenny

Evelyn Kenny lives in Ogden Utah and is the mother of four teenagers.

Evelyn graduated from Weber State University with a Bachelors Degree in Art with an emphasis in sculpture and educational design. In addition to her interest in pumpkin carving, she also enjoys making animal sculptures out of clay, sewing, and drawing.

Currently, Evelyn works as a free-lance artist and ceramic mold-maker. She is also a volunteer at a local high-school, helping Ed Palmer in the ceramics department and works on sets for school plays.

Contents

Carving Instructions

Cut the lid or the bottom of the pumpkin.

For a small pumpkin, measure at least a 4"-diameter hole for the lid; a larger pumpkin needs at least a 6"- to 8"-diameter hole.

Use the larger size saw tool or a knife to cut out the lid or the bottom of your pumpkin. Cut the lid at an angle, as it provides a ledge for the lid to rest on. Also, cut a key in the lid of your pumpkin as diagramed, to allow easy alignment when replacing the lid.

DIAGRAM

Remove the goo!

Scoop out the seeds and strings first; then, using a scraping tool, scrape out the inside lining of the pumpkin. The walls of the pumpkin should be about 1" thick. To gauge the thickness, poke a straight pin through the wall and measure how far it goes in.

Transfer the pattern to the pumpkin.

Align the most significant parts of the design in the proper position on the surface of the pumpkin. To allow the pattern to lie closer to the round surface of the pumpkin, make cuts from the corners of the pattern towards the center, then pin or tape the pattern to the pumpkin. Little pins used to hold corn on the cob work very well for pinning patterns to pumpkins. The double pins seem to keep the patterns from slipping or tearing. Push pins also work well. To avoid unnecessary holes in the surface of the pumpkin, place pins in centers of the cutouts or on the grooves of the pumpkin. **Supervise children, as pins and sharp tools pose potential hazards.**

Carefully punch holes along the outlines of the pattern with a poking tool. Do not punch all the way through the pumpkin; merely pierce the surface. The dots should be spaced about $1/16$" to $1/8$" apart. For small, intricate designs, space the dots close together; for more simple designs, space them further apart. Check to see that every line is transferred before removing the pattern. Remove the pattern. If you cannot easily see the punched pattern, dust the dots with flour.

Drill holes.

Before cutting the design, drill holes as

needed (such as for eyes or other small, round details). Drilling requires putting some pressure on the pumpkin. Drill first because after the pumpkin pattern has been cut, the pressure needed to drill could break the design in areas that have been weakened by cutting.

Carve the design.

Using a saw tool, gently but firmly pierce the tool straight into the pumpkin. Begin to saw from dot to dot. Generally, start from the center of the design and work your way outward. Saw at a 90-degree angle to the pumpkin. When using the saw tools, use a loose, smooth stroke. The saws work best when allowed to cut at their own speed. Intricate patterns require the smallest size saws. Do not rush.

To cut corners or angles, remove the saw and then reinsert it into the pumpkin. Do not twist or bend the saw, as this could break the blade.

Refer to the pattern to clarify which side of the cut will be removed. Most mistakes may be pinned back in place with toothpicks or pins.

Do not use the saw to poke out cut sections or wedged parts of the design. Cut bigger areas into smaller areas to allow easy removal of cutout parts. Be sure the pieces are completely cut free; then use the eraser end of a pencil, the end of the poking tool, or your fingers to gently push the pieces out.

Placing the candle.

Insert a candle into a candleholder designed for pumpkins (see page 11), or place it on a piece of foil inside the pumpkin towards the rear. On the top of the pumpkin, locate the place directly over the candle by lighting the candle and then placing the lid on the pumpkin for a few moments. The smoke from the candle will mark the spot where the chimney should be cut. Cut a 1"-diameter hole on the top of the pumpkin over the candle for the chimney. This will allow the air to circulate and prevent your candle from burning out or producing excess smoke.

Lighting the candle.

For pumpkins with lids, tip the pumpkin slightly and light the candle. This will help you avoid burning your fingers. For pumpkins with bottom cutouts, the candleholder can be mounted in a cut piece of pumpkin or placed in a household candleholder or perhaps a metal jar lid. Light the candle first; then place the pumpkin over it. **Be Careful with matches and candles. Supervise children.**

For posterity!

Take pictures of your artistic creation.

Keys to Classy Pumpkin Carving

1. Choose a good pumpkin to suit your design. As patterns may be enlarged or reduced on a photocopy machine, take a careful look at the complexity of the design and match difficult ones to bigger, smoother, flatter pumpkins. Get fresh pumpkins without bruises. It may help to take your patterns with you when purchasing pumpkins.

2. If you have the opportunity to pick your pumpkin right from the vine, leave 2" to 3" of vine on the stem. This will allow the pumpkin to stay fresh longer. Be careful when handling the stems. If the stem breaks, it will not keep as long. Never buy a pumpkin without a stem.

3. Acquire and learn how to use the best tools you can find. It is recommended that you use a scraper, little saws, drills, and pokers to transfer the patterns to the pumpkin.

4. Beginners should start with big, easy shapes and simple patterns. After you develop skill and control of the tools, you may confidently switch to more intricate designs and smaller cutouts.

5. Fit your pattern to your pumpkin. Since paper is flat and pumpkins are round, patterns can become distorted. Ensure that outlying pattern parts do not become too close together or overlap as the pattern wraps around the pumpkin. Patterns can be shortened the following ways:

Where a row of small decorative cutouts becomes too long, simply leave a few out without seriously altering the effect of the design.

PATTERN AS IS   **PATTERN WITH ALTERATIONS**

Long cutouts can be compressed by making an accordion fold in the pattern.

PATTERN AS IS   **PATTERN WITH ALTERATIONS**

6. Rub vegetable oil or petroleum jelly onto freshly cut areas to delay ageing.

7. Once carved, your pumpkin will only keep two-to-five days. Ideally, carve your pumpkin the day before you plan on displaying it. Refrigeration helps keep pumpkins fresh. To refresh a shriveled design, soak pumpkin in water for two-to-eight hours or more. Be careful not to oversoak, as cracking may occur. Dry off pumpkin, as standing water will soften it.

8. To make your own poking tool, make a handle from a rounded piece of wood, such as a broom handle, etc. Clamp the handle in a bench vise and drive a nail into the wood until it is seated firmly. Clip off the head of the nail with pliers or wire cutters, leaving a ¼" length. Use a grinder or a whetstone to sharpen to a point.

9. One of the simplest tools for scraping is a canning jar lid. Also, a potter's trimming tool is ideal for scraping as well. It has a short sturdy handle and an effective cutting edge (yet not too sharp for children) and is easy to control. The loop of the trimming tool cuts thin shavings away from the inside of the pumpkin.

10. Practice your technique on extra pumpkins. Also, use the patterns on pages 20, 70, 87, 89, 91, 93, and 95 on watermelons, honeydews, or canteloupes for year-round carving entertainment.

11. The more difficult patterns are marked with a .

Tools

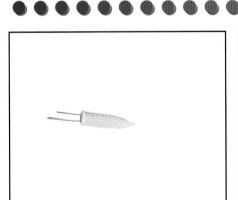

POKING TOOL

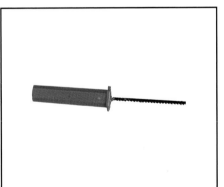

SAW TOOL

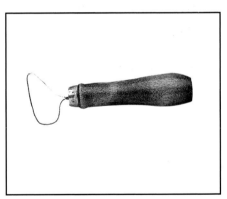

POTTER'S TOOL

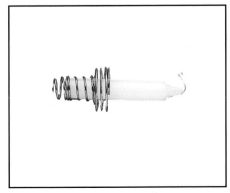

CANDLEHOLDER

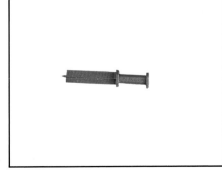

DRILL

Creepy Cauldron

13

Ghastly Grimace

PEARS: A COUNTRY CAFE

Crazy Face

Drill the eyeholes first. Cut
the tongue starting at the
center. Cut the upper lip last.

Phreeky Phantom

**Work the mouth last,
cutting it in sections to avoid
breaking teeth.**

Gobble Gobble

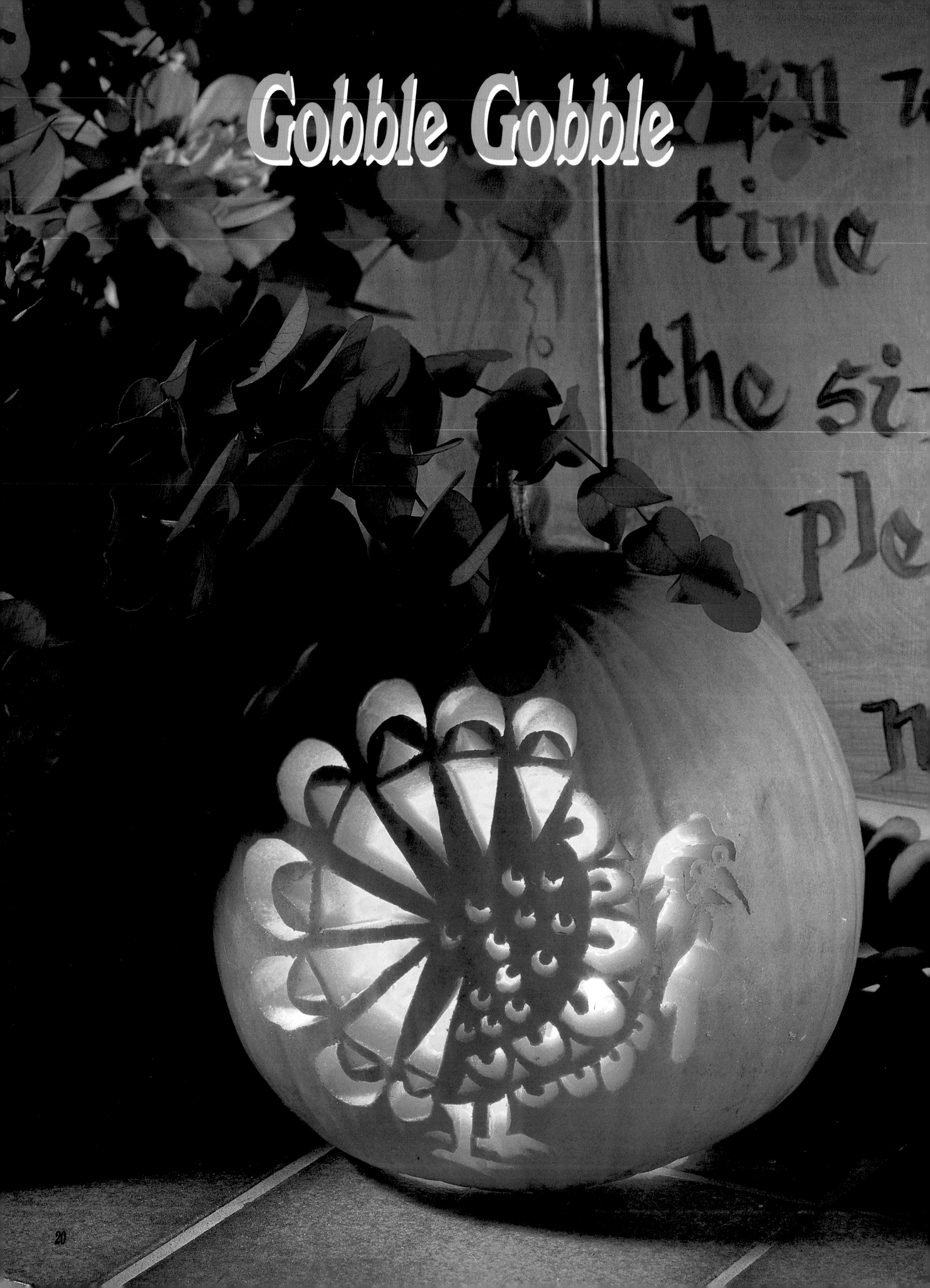

Drill the eyeholes first. Work
from the center out. Trace
and cut carefully as this is a
complicated pattern.

Head Hunter

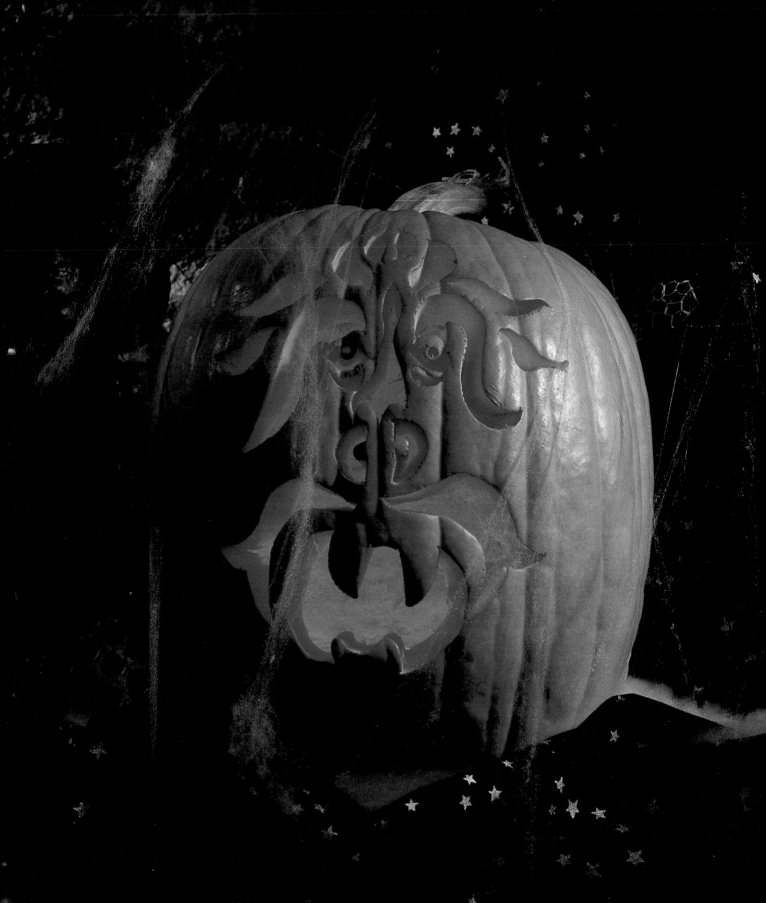

Goblin Growl

Jazz Scat Cat

Be sure to leave enough space between the eye openings for support.

29

This pattern really looks great
because of the intricate details.
Be sure to leave enough pumpkin
between the openings for support.

Vampire

33

Cut out the centers of the eyes first. Where details are close together, as in the eye area, work from one side to the other.

Conjuring Bat

Goodtime Jack

Leo Drool

Cut eyes and mouth last.

Flameburst Face

47

Maniac

Cut small areas first and
large areas last.

Drill the eyeholes first; then, cut small areas next. Cut around entire mouth and take it out in sections.

Snakey Squash

Cut small areas first.
Work mouth last.

Batty Wings

Gypsy

Crescent Moon

Stressed Squash

Distressed

The Masque

Skull & Crossbones

Goofy Gremlin

Cut mouth last.

Nautical Nightmare

71

Viper

Spikes

**Drill the eyes first.
Cut small areas next. Cut
around entire mouth, carefully removing it in sections.**

75

Perky Pumpkin

Cut out tongue last, starting
with the center piece that
hangs down.

Lips In Stitches

Cut mouth last.

The Jovial Joker

Witchypooh

83

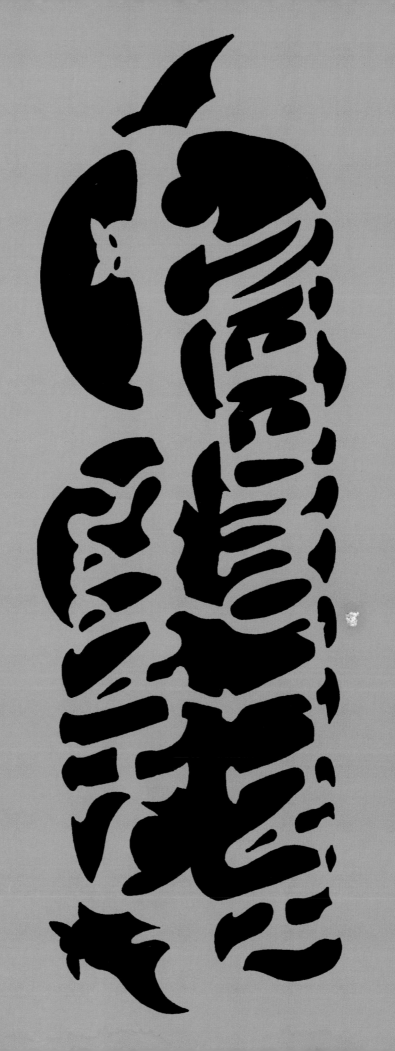

Fancy Watermelon

1. Trace the end pattern or basket handle (page 89) patterns onto the melon.

2. Use the saw tools to cut the inside parts of the patterns.

3. Cut around the first openings, maintaining about ¼" distance from the openings to make the outer edges of the design. You may wish to trace the outer design also.

4. Cut the edge scallop to allow room for the edge designs. Connect the edge scallop with the outer cuts of the end pattern or basket handle pattern.

5. Trace the edge designs (page 89) inside the scallops, or draw them gently with a pencil.

6. Cut the edge designs using the saw tool.

7. Use a melon-baller to remove the flesh from the melon.

END PATTERNS

Trace and cut end openings first.

Then cut the outer edge around the first openings.

Cut scallops, connecting the end scallop with the outer edge of the end design or basket handle.

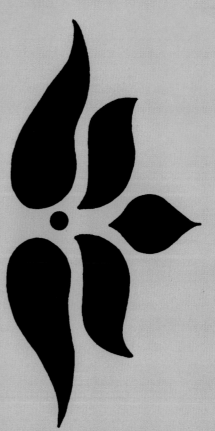

Watermelon Basket

**WATERMELON
HANDLE PATTERN**

**WATERMELON
EDGE PATTERN**
(Select the ones you will
use and repeat as
necessary around the
edge. Add or subtract,
enlarge or reduce to fit as
melons vary greatly in
size and shape.)

**WATERMELON
HANDLE PATTERN**

89

Floral Cantaloupe

Carefully consider the size and shape of the melon prior to tracing or cutting.

1. Align pattern and trace outlines with pattern poking tool.

2. Drill and cut inner holes first.

3. Gently separate top of melon.

4. Scoop out seeds and make melon balls.

5. Cut decorative edges.

Fancy Cantaloupe

1. Slice off the top of the melon.

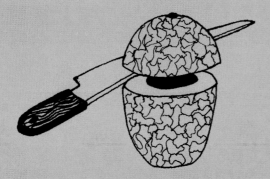

2. Transfer the desired pattern around the top of the melon, repeating as necessary to cover the melon.

3. Cut inner design openings first.

4. Scallop outer edges of design last.

5. Scoop out seeds and make cantaloupe balls.

It is recommended that you transfer the pattern with the pattern poking tool, as the netted texture of the cantaloupe is difficult to trace on.

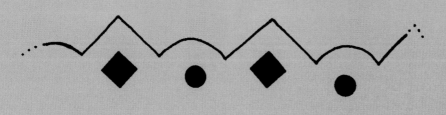

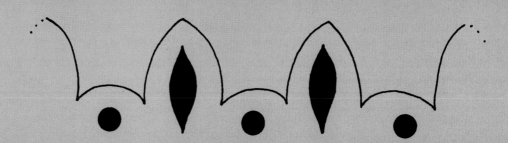

Melon Bird

1. Tape a pencil to an appropriate sized glass, can, or similar object. Place the melon against the point of the pencil. Rotate the melon, lightly tracing a line just above the midpoint of the melon. This will help to align the pattern.

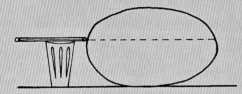

2. Using the pattern poking tool, transfer the pattern sections to the melon.

3. Connect segments at * or add extra wing segments to adjust for the size of your melon.

4. The tail lines up with other pattern sections on the line above the mid-point of the melon.

5. Cut the design using the saw tool.

6. Use a melon-baller to remove the flesh from the melon.

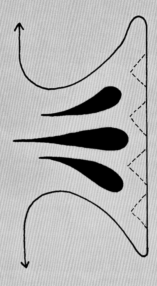

METRIC EQUIVALENCE CHART

MM-Millimetres   CM-Centimetres

INCHES TO MILLIMETRES AND CENTIMETRES

INCHES	MM	CM	INCHES	CM	INCHES	CM
1/8	3	0.9	9	22.9	30	76.2
1/4	6	0.6	10	25.4	31	78.7
3/8	10	1.0	11	27.9	32	81.3
1/2	13	1.3	12	30.5	33	83.8
5/8	16	1.6	13	33.0	34	86.4
3/4	19	1.9	14	35.6	35	88.9
7/8	22	2.2	15	38.1	36	91.4
1	25	2.5	16	40.6	37	94.0
1 1/4	32	3.2	17	43.2	38	96.5
1 1/2	38	3.8	18	45.7	39	99.1
1 3/4	44	4.4	19	48.3	40	101.6
2	51	5.1	20	50.8	41	104.1
2 1/2	64	6.4	21	53.3	42	106.7
3	76	7.6	22	55.9	43	109.2
3 1/2	89	8.9	23	58.4	44	111.8
4	102	10.2	24	61.0	45	114.3
4 1/2	114	11.4	25	63.5	46	116.8
5	127	12.7	26	66.0	47	119.4
6	152	15.2	27	68.6	48	121.9
7	178	17.8	28	71.1	49	124.5
8	203	20.3	29	73.7	50	127.0

INDEX